Journey Along a River

The Ganges

Jen Green

WAYLAND

This book is a differentiated text version of *A River Journey The Ganges* by Rob Bowden.

This edition first published in 2009 by Wayland
Copyright © 2009 Wayland

Wayland
338 Euston Road
London NW1 3BH

Wayland
Level 17/207 Kent Street
Sydney NSW 2000

Editor: Victoria Brooker
Designer: Stephen Prosser

Brtish Cataloguing in Publication Data
 Green, Jen.
   The Ganges. -- (Journey along a river)
   1. Ganges River (India and Bangladesh)--Juvenile
   literature. 2. Ganges River Valley (India and Bangladesh)--
   Juvenile literature.
   I. Title II. Series

   915.4'1-dc22

ISBN: 978 0 7502 5872 2

Printed in China

Wayland is a division of Hachette Children's Books,
an Hachette UK company.
www.hachette.co.uk

The website addresses (URLs) included in this book were valid at the time of going to press. However, because of the nature of the Internet, it is possible that some addresses may have changed, or sites may have changed or closed down since publication. While the author and Publisher regret any inconvenience this may cause readers, no responsibility for any such changes can be accepted by either the author or the Publisher.

The maps in this book use a conical projection,and so the indicator for North on the main map is only approximate.

Picture Acknowledgements
Cover and page 18 Eye Ubiquitous/David Cumming; title page,Still Pictures/Gill Noti; 3 Impact/Charles Coates; 5 Jane Hawkins; 6 Ecoscene/Robert Weight; Hutchinson/Dave Brinicombe; 8 Axiom/Chris Caldecott, inset Associated Press; 9 Axiom/Ian Cumming; 10 Rex/Jerome Hutin; 11 Rex/ Jerome Hutin; 12 Hutchinson/Andrew Hill; 13 Network/Mike Goldwater, inset Dinodia; 14 Indian Tourist Board; 15 left Eye Ubiqitous/David Cumming, right Hutchinson/Dave Brinicombe; 16 Oxford Scientific Films/Kenneth Day, inset Still Pictures/Rachus Chundawat; 17 Trip/R Lal; 19 Eye Ubiquitous/David Cumming; bottom Rex Features/Simon Wellock ; 20 Trip/H Rogers; 22 Trip/Dinodia; 23 Dinodia/Anil A. Dave; inset Axiom/Jim Holmes; 24 Associated Press/John McConnico, inset Impact/Charles Coates; 25 Associated Press/ Amit Bhargava, inset Axiom/ Paul Quayle; 26 Reuters/Popperfoto; 27 Reuters/Jayanta Shaw; 28 Eye Ubuiquitous/ David Cumming, bottom Impact/Charles Coates; 30 Dinodia/ RK Makharia; 31 Trip/F Good, bottom Eye Ubiquitous/Bennett Dean; 32 & 33 Suvendu Chatterjee; 34 Associated Press/ Bikas Das; 35 Eye Ubiquitous/David Cumming; 36 & 37 Suvendu Chatterjee, bottom HWPL; 38 Still Pictures/Gil Moti; 39 Science Photo Library; 40 Popperfoto/Rafique Rahman; 41 Still Pictures/Shehzad Noorani; 42 Eye Ubuquitous/David Cumming, inset Still Pictures/Gunter Ziesler; 43 Still Pictures/Gil Noti, inset Still Pictures/ Shehzad Noorani; 44 Still Pictures/Jorgen Schytte, inset Impact/Alastair Guild.

Contents

Words in **bold** can be found in the glossary on page 47.

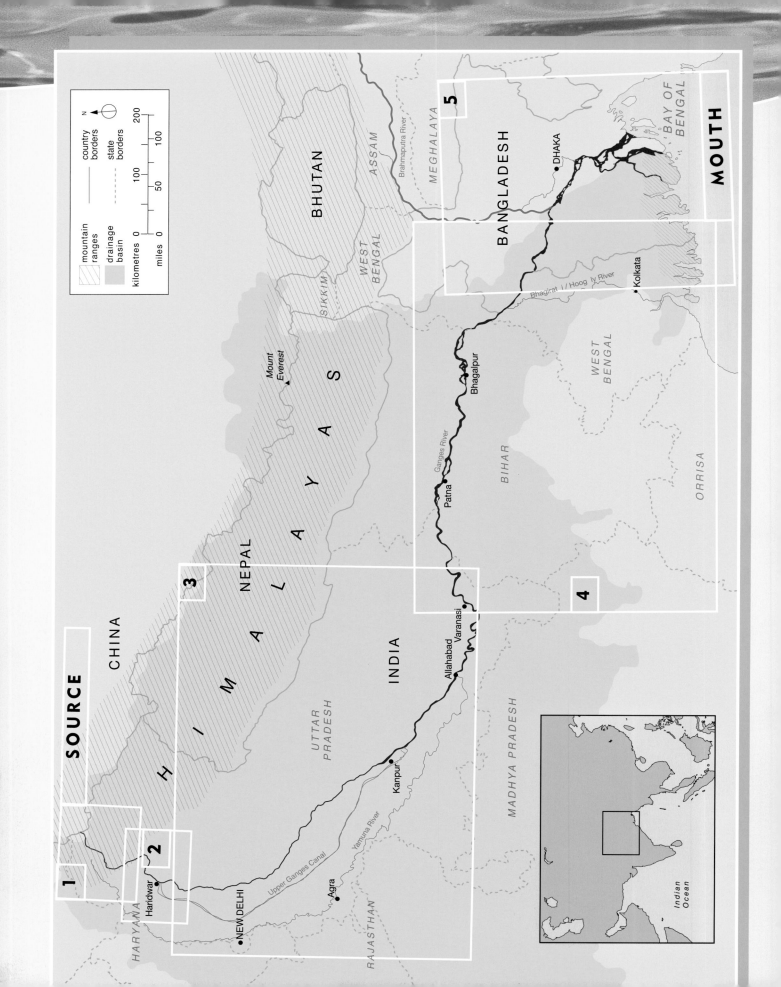

SOURCE

MOUTH

mountain ranges
drainage basin

country borders
state borders

N

kilometres 0   50   100   200
miles   0   50   100

1

2

3

4

5

CHINA

BHUTAN

ASSAM

Brahmaputra River

MEGHALAYA

BANGLADESH

DHAKA

BAY OF BENGAL

WEST BENGAL

SIKKIM

Mount Everest

Bhagirat I / Hoog ly River

Kolkata

H I M A L A Y A S

NEPAL

Bhagalpur

Ganges River

Patna

WEST BENGAL

BIHAR

ORRISA

Allahabad
Varanasi

INDIA

UTTAR PRADESH

Kanpur

MADHYA PRADESH

Yamuna River

Upper Ganges Canal

HARYANA

Haridwar

NEW DELHI

Agra

RAJASTHAN

Indian Ocean

Your guide to the river

Using maps

The River Ganges is one of the world's most famous rivers. It flows for 2,507 kilometres across southern Asia. More than 350 million people live along its banks. To most of those people the river is sacred. The map on page 4 shows the whole length of the Amazon River. The white squares show how our journey along the river has been divided into six chapters.

Map references

Each chapter has a map showing the part of the river we have reached. The numbered boxes show where places of interest are found.

The Journey Ahead

We are on an epic journey, following the River Ganges from the **source** to the mouth. Our journey begins in an ice cave high in the Himalayan mountains in northern India. From here the Ganges flows 2,507 kilometres right across India and Bangladesh to the ocean.

At first the river drops very steeply, tumbling through sheer **gorges** and over waterfalls. Later it slows down. We cross a vast, fertile plain and explore some of India's amazing cities, such as Varanasi and Patna.

We enter Bangladesh at the Farakka Barrage, one of the few **dams** on the river. The Ganges is vital to farming in Bangladesh. Near the end of our journey we reach the Ganges **delta** – the world's biggest delta. Our journey ends where the Ganges empties into the Indian Ocean.

Our journey starts on foot in the mighty Himalayas. You'll need your hiking boots!

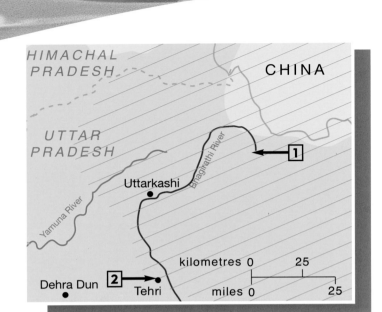

1. The Ganges headwaters

The start of a river is called the source. The Ganges begins high in the Himalayas. Here, many streams and young rivers pour down from the mountains, fed by melting ice. The **headwaters** of a river are all the streams and young rivers that join the river near the source.

▼ **Icy water drains into the Ganges from glaciers high in the Himalayas.**

The Gangotri glacier

The Gangotri glacier MAP REF 1 is considered to be the source of the Ganges. This vast glacier lies at over 4,000 metres above sea level. It covers an area of almost 200 square kilometres. Scientists believe that the ice in the glacier is at least four 400 years old.

A glacier is like a frozen river of ice. It is made from unmelted snow, which gets packed down to form ice. The huge weight of the ice sets the glacier very slowly flowing downhill.

We visit the source, where **meltwater** trickles from an ice cave in the lowest part of the glacier. This icy stream, called the Bhagirathi River, becomes the Ganges later on. We follow as it tumbles downhill. As we descend we meet Hindu pilgrims coming up on foot and by pony.

A sacred river

Of all the world's rivers, the Ganges is probably the most sacred. It is particularly holy for Hindus, who call it the Ganga. The pilgrims we passed are coming to visit the source. Hinduism

▲ **This Hindu holy man is called a sadhu. He has travelled barefoot to the source of the Ganges.**

is the main religion in India. There are also many Muslims, and also Buddhists, Sikhs and Christians.

Hindu stories

Many legends are told about the Ganges. One Hindu myth tells how the river came to flow on Earth. The gods ordered the goddess Ganga, a river living in the heavens, to fall to Earth. Ganga was angry and began crashing to Earth. The Lord Shiva caught her in his long hair and tied her in knots. When she was calm, he untied his hair. Now Ganga tumbles gently down from the Himalayas across India to the ocean.

▲ Part of the Himalayas in India.

▶ These children were injured by the Uttarkashi earthquake in 1991.

Top of the world

The Himalayas are the world's highest mountains. They stretch for nearly 3,000 kilometres through Pakistan, India, Nepal, China and Bhutan. The part of India where we are travelling has mountains over 7,000 metres high.

India and Asia are now joined together, but they were once separated by a vast sea. Upheaval deep below Earth's surface gradually pushed the two landmasses together. Over millions of years, they inched closer. When they finally collided, the border zone crumpled upward to form the Himalayas.

Mountains that form in this way are called **fold mountains**. India and Asia are still pushing against one another, so the Himalayas are still rising. Mount Everest, the world's highest mountain at 8,848 metres, is getting about 2.5 centimetres taller each year!

Earthquakes

Enormous pressure builds up as landmasses push together. Sometimes the pressure is released as rocks shift in a violent jolt called an **earthquake**. Earthquakes make buildings collapse and can trigger **landslides**. In built-up areas they can kill thousands of people.

In October 1991, a massive earthquake struck the town of Uttarkashi near Haridwar. It killed over 1,000 people and destroyed 42,000 homes.

Hill farming

Most people in this part of India work as farmers. There is little flat land. But the farmers here have cut steps called terraces into the hillsides to make small, flat fields. Stone walls hold back the soil. The terraces collect rainwater, and also help to prevent the soil from slipping downhill. As we climb, we pass cereals, **pulses** and vegetables growing together on the terraces. This system is called intercropping. It helps the soil to remain fertile and spreads the work of farming through the year. It also helps to prevent one crop from being destroyed by pests or disease.

▼ **A 'staircase' of terraced fields on a hillside in northern India.**

The Tehri Dam

India needs massive amounts of energy to power its factories and cities. Energy from fast-flowing water can be used to produce a type of electricity called **hydroelectricity**. When a hydroelectric plant is built, the river is dammed to control the flow. An artificial lake called a **reservoir** forms behind the dam.

In 1961, a site for a new dam was chosen near the town of Tehri MAP REF 2. A dam towering 260 metres high was planned. Engineers said the valley behind would be flooded by an enormous reservoir. The building work would create thousands of jobs. River water would surge past giant wheels called turbines to produce electricity.

For and against

Work on the Tehri Dam began in the 1970s, but then a fierce debate broke out. Supporters of the project said the dam would provide a huge amount of energy while causing little pollution. It would

▶ **Work on the Tehri Dam began in the 1970s.**

▼ **This valley will be flooded by the dam.**

help prevent flooding, and the reservoir would provide water for farming. But some scientists were against the dam.

The scientists were worried that the dam had been planned in a earthquake zone. If another major earthquake struck nearby, the dam could crack. A wall of water could sweep downriver to devastate cities in the valley below.

Protests

Local people were also worried. Around 100,000 people would have to move to make way for the reservoir. They feared they would not be given land or money to replace their lost homes and farms. Some

▲ **The reservoir flooded the lands of farming families like these.**

scientists claimed that **silt** from the river would block the plant's turbines within about 30 years.

During the 1990s, building work on the dam stopped because of protests. An 81-year-old man called Sunderlal Bahuguna refused to eat for 56 days, until the government promised to look into all the problems. However, the government later gave the project the go-ahead, and work restarted in 2001. When the dam was finished, the lake began to form. In 2005, the lake swamped the town of Tehri.

Seasons of the Ganges

Between November and February, the **climate** of this region is fairly dry. Rainfall is low and the Ganges flows slowly. By March, the air is warming up. Snow and ice start to melt in the high mountains. Meltwater swells the Ganges and its tributaries – the smaller rivers that join it.

This part of Asia lies in the path of changeable winds called **monsoons**. Monsoon winds bring very heavy rain in certain seasons. In late June, the monsoon rains arrive. Heavy rain can fall for days on end. Rainwater fills the Ganges, causing flooding in many places along the river.

Disappearing forests

We descend through forested slopes above the Ganges. Parts of these forests have been cleared to make way for new roads and mines. Local people also cut down some trees to burn as fuel or to create new fields. When forests are cut down it is called **deforestation**.

Wearing away

Rocks and soil are naturally worn away by rain, wind and ice. This is called **erosion**. Erosion usually happens quite slowly, but deforestation can speed it up. The roots of forest trees anchor the soil and prevent it from washing away. When trees are cut down, the loose soil washes away after heavy rain, particularly on steep hillsides. Lower down, soil can clog the river and slow it down, which increases the risk of flooding.

Deforestation can trigger landslides. In August 1998, heavy monsoon rains caused major landslides in this region. Homes, roads, farms and animals were swept away, and nearly 300 people died.

◀ **Sunderlal Bahuguna is a leader of the Chipko Movement. He also fought against the Tehri Dam.**

▲ This path by the Ganges has flooded during the monsoon.

▲ This mountain road has been hit by a landslide. Bushes and trees have been swept away.

The Chipko Movement

The people of these hills know all about deforestation and the risks it brings. In the 1970s, local people formed a protest group to protect their forests from the loggers. It was called the Chipko Movement. Chipko means 'to cling' in **Hindi**, a local language. Some protesters clung to trees to prevent them being cut down.

The protests were reported in newspapers in many countries. The Chipko movement became famous all over the world. The protesters changed the Indian government's view and led to bans on logging in the region.

We are leaving the high mountains. The Ganges is now deep enough for us to use an inflatable raft. Hang on tight!

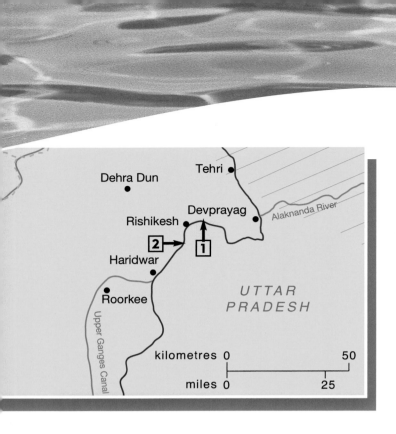

2. The Upper Ganges

On our raft we experience the river's power. We plunge downstream toward Haridwar. The small town of Devprayag is a landmark on our journey. Here, the Bhagirathi River joins the Alaknanda River. Our river changes its name – from now on it is called the Ganges.

▼ **Rafting down the Ganges towards Haridwar.**

▲ Two rivers meet at the tiny temple town of Devprayag, high in the hills.

▲ Pilgrims use these ghats to bathe. You can see the same ghats in the photograph on the left.

Where rivers meet

A place where two rivers meet is called a **confluence**. For Hindus, any confluence is sacred, and the meeting of these two rivers is especially holy.

The banks at Devprayag are lined with stepped platforms called **ghats**. Pilgrims use the ghats to bathe in the Ganges. They believe the water will wash away their sins and guide them towards **Nirvana** – a state of spiritual freedom.

A holy place

Hindus who live close to the Ganges often bathe at dawn and dusk. They offer gifts of flowers and food. Holy men called sadhus spend their lives visiting shrines in India, including along the Ganges.

Over the rapids

Our raft trip down the Upper Ganges is one of the wildest white-water rides on Earth! The river roars as it surges through narrow gorges and over foaming **rapids**. The rapids form where the water crashes over boulders on the river-bed.

We fight the rapids as we plunge downstream for many kilometres. The roar of the water is deafening. But we're not worried. Our guides are experienced and have made this trip many times before. On board, our food, tents and other gear are sealed in waterproof bags. At night we camp on sand banks by the river. These have formed along the inside bends of the river. Here, the current slows and the river drops sand and stones.

Rajaji National Park

We pass through Rajaji National Park MAP REF 1. This park covers 820 square kilometres. It was set up in the 1980s to protect the **environment**. The park has about 50 types of mammals, over 300 different birds, and many fish, reptiles and butterflies.

Four islands on the Ganges lie within the park. We leave the raft to look around. There are herons, ducks and cormorants. But we have to watch our

step, as there are also many snakes! Back on the raft we pass by female elephants with their babies. Hidden in the long grass may be a tiger! You might even spot a leopard snoozing in a tree.

Nomads of the park

Rajaji National Park is home to the Gujjars, a **nomadic** people who are buffalo herders. Throughout the year, the Gujjars move their buffaloes between different mountain pastures where there is fresh grazing.

► **Elephants enjoy a cooling mud bath on the banks of the Ganges.**

▼ **Cormorants perch on a tree by the river in the park.**

As they pass through the park, the Gujjars use the plants and trees for animal feed, fuel wood and to build temporary shelters. They may also kill park wildlife for food. The Gujjars have used this land for centuries, long before the park was formed. But now the park authorities want to prevent them from passing through. They say the Gujjars and their herds harm the environment.

Ecotourism

At Ganga Banks MAP REF 2 we reach one of the most environmentally-friendly hotels in India. This resort is built from local materials, but not a single tree was cut down to build it. Some rooms even

▲ **A group of Gujjar women by a temporary shelter, built from forest materials.**

have living trees growing through them! As tourists are becoming more aware of environmental problems, more people are choosing holidays that don't harm the natural world. This type of tourism is called **ecotourism**.

Ganga Banks

At Ganga Banks we see many environmentally-friendly practices. Waste water is used to water the lawns. Food waste is turned into compost. **Solar energy** is used for cooking and heating. All these practices are kind to the environment.

▲ **Bathing ghats on the river at Haridwar.**

▶ **Priests float candles on the water at dusk.**

Holy places

We float downstream to Rishikesh, a centre for meditation and yoga. Yoga is a form of physical exercise that also refreshes the mind. Rishikesh is the perfect place to relax if you are tired or worried and anxious. The town has about 70,000 people and several centres for meditation.

As we continue, we leave the mountains behind and enter a flat plain. By the time we reach the city of Haridwar, just 24 kilometres downstream, the river has slowed as it flows through flattish land.

'Gateway to the gods'

Haridwar is about three times the size of Rishikesh. Its name means 'gateway to the gods'. Bathing ghats line the river. The current is still quite strong here, so pilgrims grip chains fixed to the ghats so they don't get swept away while bathing. In the evening priests offer prayers and float little candles on the water.

The Upper Ganges Canal

For centuries, farmers living by the Ganges have used river water to wet their fields. This is called **irrigation**. In the 1840s, a **canal** was built at Haridwar to divert water for farming. The canal was also used by boats.

The Upper Ganges Canal is nearly 500 kilometres long. At the time it was the largest irrigation system in the world. People still come to marvel at the **aqueducts** – bridges that transport other rivers over the canal.

The town of Roorkee lies on the canal not far from Haridwar. Before the canal was built Roorkee was just a few houses. The canal provided new job opportunities and 150,000 people now live in the town.

The railway arrives

Two hundred years ago, boats could sail the Ganges River all year round. Paddle-steamers cruised up and down the river. After the canal was built **navigation** became more difficult because there was less water in the river.

▲ **The Upper Ganges Canal is an amazing feat of engineering.**

However, as the railways were built, a new form of transport appeared. Railways soon became India's main form of transport.

India's railway network has 63,000 kilometres of track, 8,000 trains and nearly 7,000 stations. With more than 1.4 million workers, the Indian Railways are one of the biggest employers in the world.

We now board a slow train as we follow the river to the ancient city of Varanasi.

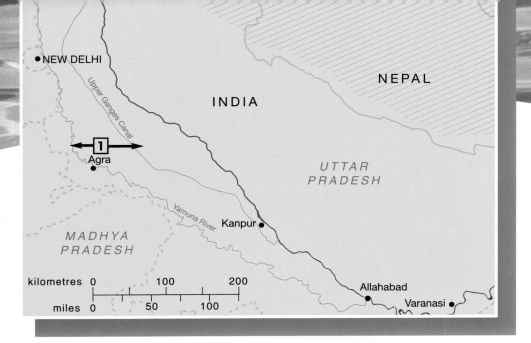

3. The Middle Ganges

With the mountains behind us, we enter a region of flat, fertile farmland. This is one of the most densely populated parts of India. When we reach the riverside cities of Kanpur, Allahabad and Varanasi we leave the train to view the sights.

▼ **The crops, plants and animals of the plains are very different to those of the hills.**

A fertile plain

The Himalayas look rugged, but they are actually made of fairly soft rocks. These wear away easily in heavy monsoon rains. Over 1,000 tonnes of rock and soil are worn from each square kilometre of mountain land in a year. Much of this rocky debris ends up in the Ganges, where the river grinds it into fine silt. When the river floods, it spreads silt over the surrounding valley. Over millions of years, the silt has built up to form deep, fertile soil.

Farming the doab

An area called the doab MAP REF 1 lies between the Ganges and the Yamuna River to the south. Doab means 'land between rivers'. For centuries, people have farmed the deep soil enriched by silt. Local

▲ Wheat and barley are grown in the doab. Here a crop is being dried before it is stored.

farmers also add cattle dung and plant waste to fertilise the soil. A wide variety of crops can be grown on the doab. In days gone by, several crops were often grown together. This is an example of intercropping. Or different crops were grown each year. The crops used different **nutrients**, so the soil remained fertile.

Finding enough water for crops is a problem in the long, dry season. Farmers used to draw water from wells to irrigate their fields. After the mid-1800s, the Upper Ganges Canal transformed farming in the area. However, an even bigger change followed in the 1960s – a change called the Green Revolution.

The Green Revolution

In the 1960s, the Indian government was worried that farmers would not be able to produce enough food for everyone. The government introduced new farming methods to increase food production, and opened up new areas for farming.

The new methods included using new strains of wheat and rice that would produce bumper crops. These are called High Yield Varieties, or HYVs for short. The new crops were stronger than traditional seeds.

The new crops had a shorter growing season. This meant that farmers could grow two crops a year instead of one. The first crop grew during the monsoon, but the second came up in the dry season. So farmers needed new methods of watering. The answer was to improve irrigation.

Benefits

New wells called tubewells were sunk. These are long plastic tubes which reach water deep underground. The water is then pumped to the surface. In 1960 India had just 3,000 tubewells. By 1990 there were over six million!

The new farming methods were very successful. They produced record harvests of rice and wheat. In just ten years, India was producing enough of these crops to feed its people and also sell some abroad.

▼ **Irrigation, especially from tubewells, has transformed farming in India.**

▲ ► **The new farming methods need chemicals and modern equipment. Poor farmers cannot afford these and they can harm the environment.**

Drawbacks

Not everyone benefited from the Green Revolution. To succeed, farmers needed money for HYV seeds, tubewells and also chemicals. But many farmers could not afford them. Some farmers who had rented their fields were turned off their land by landowners eager to profit from the new methods. So many poor farmers became poorer, and some were forced to leave their farms and look for work in the cities.

HYV seeds can cope with dry conditions. But they can be badly hit by insect pests or disease. They also need more weeding. So farmers started using chemical sprays to control disease, weeds and pests. But these chemicals harm the environment when they leak into the water or soil.

The coming of HYVs has also reduced the variety of crops that are grown. For example, around 50 varieties of rice are grown today, but in the past there were many thousands of varieties. This can mean that crops are at greater risk of pests and disease.

▲ ▶ **Untreated sewage and dead animals pollute the Ganges.**

A dirty river

We reach Kanpur, where leather and textile factories line the river banks. These industries are important, but cause a lot of pollution. Each year an incredible 135,000 tonnes of dye, bleach and other harmful chemicals are emptied into the river.

Kanpur is not the only city to cause pollution. Over 200 million tonnes of waste from factories spill into the river daily. The water is also polluted by chemicals from farming, and animal carcasses being dumped here. People also cremate (burn) the bodies of dead relatives on the ghats. The ashes go into the water. However, the biggest single cause of pollution is sewage. Over 1,300 million tonnes of it enters the river daily.

Pollution and health

People rely on Ganges water for washing, cooking and even drinking. Water pollution presents a serious health risk to the people of Kanpur and other cities along the Ganges.

Cholera and **typhoid** are serious diseases which are spread by polluted water. Across India, nearly 70 per cent of all water supplies are polluted. Throughout our journey, we are being very careful to boil, filter or purify all water before we drink it.

▲ **Hindus believe it is especially holy to be cremated by the Ganges.**

▶ **A farmer washes his buffalo in the river.**

A clean-up plan

In 1985, the Indian government launched the Ganges Action Plan, which aimed to clean up waste before it entered the river. New sewage pumping stations were built, and people were taught how to take better care of the environment.

The scheme cost over 330 million US dollars, but has not been a success. Many projects are unfinished, others don't work properly. Sewage treatment plants don't work at all during power cuts, which happen regularly. The government encouraged people not to cremate bodies by the river. But Hindus believe this practice will send the person straight to heaven, so they ignore the advice.

Since the plan came in, the amount of sewage entering the Ganges has actually doubled! Less than 20 per cent of it has been treated to make it safe.

A three-way junction

About 200 kilometres downstream from Kanpur, we reach the ancient city of Allahabad. Here the Ganges meets two other rivers of great religious importance – the Yamuna River and the mythical Saraswati River.

The Yamuna River starts high in the Himalayas like the Ganges. It is 1,370 kilometres long and flows past India's capital, New Delhi. The Yamuna adds its water to the Ganges. But the Saraswati River adds no physical water at all. Millions of devout Hindus believe in the existence of this sacred river, but geographers can find no physical trace of it at all.

▶ **Pilgrims bathe in the Ganges during the Kumbh Mela festival.**

▼ **An aerial view of the Yamuna River meeting the muddy Ganges.**

World's biggest festival

The place where the Ganges, Yamuna and the mythical Saraswati meet is sacred to Hindus. It is a very holy place to bathe. Every twelve years, Hindus gather here to celebrate the festival of Maha Kumbh Mela.

In January 2001, about 30 million Hindus gathered to celebrate the Kumbh Mela. This was the world's largest-ever gathering of people. The authorities had prepared by building a temporary city to house the pilgrims. This had 400,000 tents, 75,000 toilets and 61 access roads.

Careful preparations help people to keep safe. In 1954, 300 pilgrims were trampled to death. In 1989, over 3,000 people were lost in the huge crowds and some were never found. In 2001, special camps were set up to reunite lost people with their families.

Tourism in Varanasi

Our next stop is the ancient city of Varanasi, a centre for trade, learning, religion and crafts. The city was founded over 3,000 years ago and the local silk industry is almost as old.

With its long history, Varanasi attracts tourists from all over the world. We join tourists on an early morning boat trip to watch an ancient tradition. As the Ganges sparkles pink and gold in the light of dawn, pilgrims gather at the river to pray and bathe.

Later, we head into the bustling old city. We wander a maze of alleys and buy silk souvenirs. Finally, we take a rickshaw ride to our hotel. These three-wheeled vehicles are either powered by a small motor engine or by a human cyclist. Our hotel has great views over the Ganges. But we have to watch out for monkeys, who steal food from unwary tourists!

◀ **People gather on the ghats at Varanasi to pray and bathe at dawn.**

The caste system

Hindu society is traditionally divided into groups called **castes**. The highest caste is the Brahmins, who are priests. Next comes the Kshatriyas, officials and soldiers, and then the Vaishyas, who are traders and craftspeople.

The Shudras, who are skilled labourers, farmers and servants, are the lowest caste. But another group have even lower status, and no caste at all. These are the Dalits, who do all the work other people will not do, such as cleaning toilets and collecting rubbish. The word Dalit means 'the Oppressed'. Dalits make up about 15 per cent of India's population.

The Indian government strongly discourages caste. It is not as important as it used to be, especially in cities, where people of different castes, work, eat and socialise together. But marriage is still unusual between different castes. In the countryside, caste is still strong. Dalits are forbidden to enter Hindu temples or even use certain wells.

We now take a rowing boat and head down river to the city of Patna.

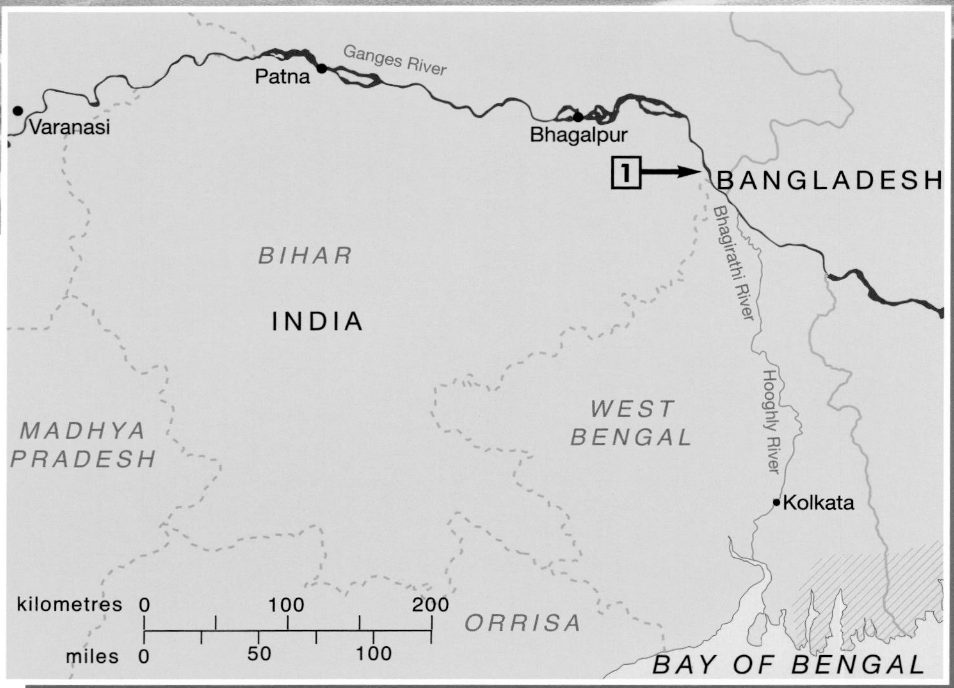

4. The Lower Ganges

Patna is the capital of Bihar state. It is also a historic city. We stop and learn more about India's history here. Then we take a side trip down the Hooghly River which branches off the Ganges to visit Kolkata, the largest city on our journey.

▼ The Sikh temple in Patna is a place of pilgrimage for Sikhs.

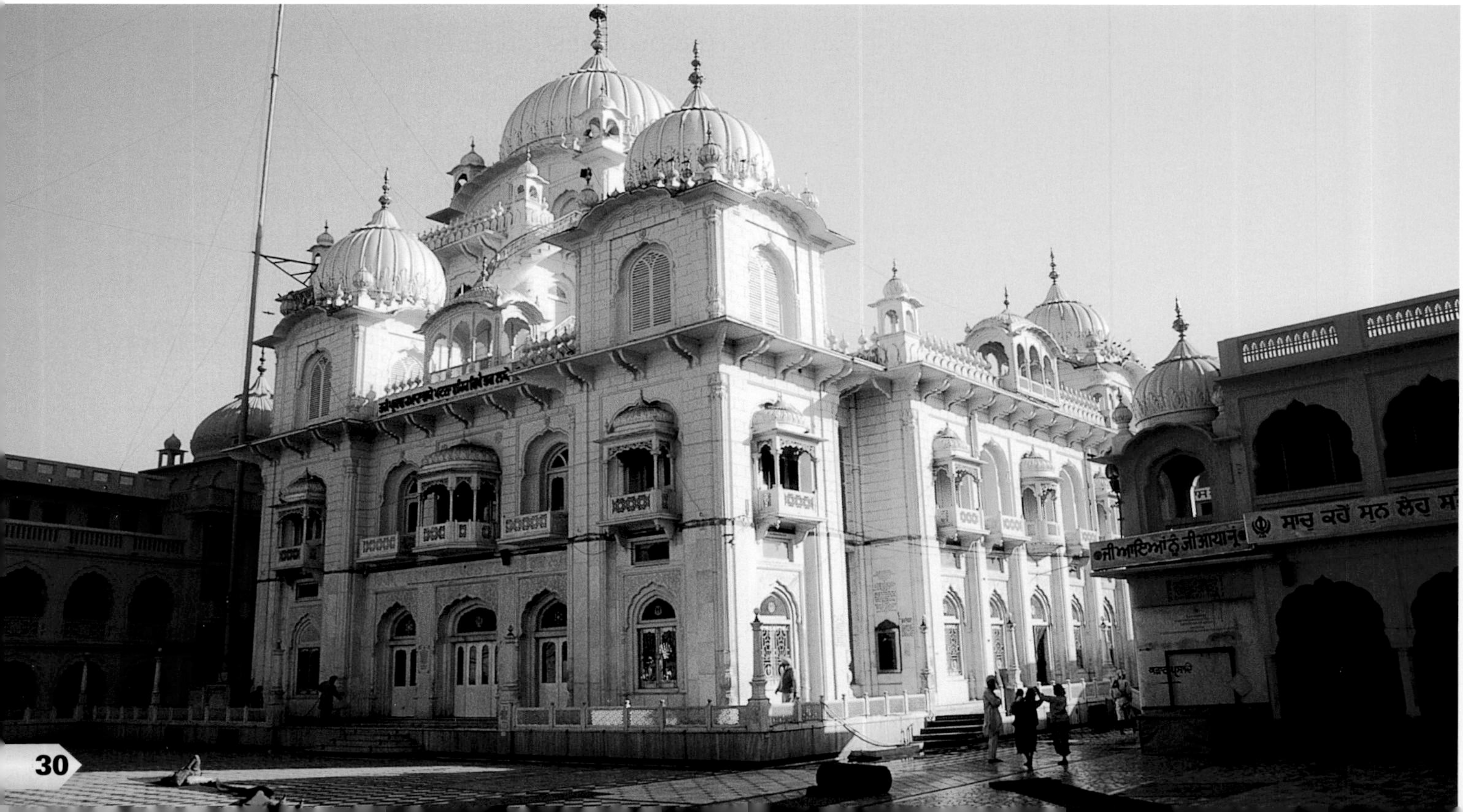

▲ **The Golghar was built to store grain. It is now a tourist attraction.**

Patna

Patna dates back to the 400s BCE. At this time it was called Pataliputra. It was the centre of several early kingdoms, but by the 600s CE it was abandoned. Later, in the 1540s, it grew up again as Patna. At this point it was ruled by a king of the Mughal Empire. The Mughals were a line of Muslim rulers who once controlled much of southern Asia.

The British took control of Patna in 1765. They ruled until 1947, when India gained independence. In Patna, the past is all around us. The Sher Shahi Mosque is a famous Muslim shrine. The Sikh temple of Harmandirji is a holy place for Sikhs.

A large, dome-shaped building called the Golghar is another landmark. The British built it to store grain in the 1780s. It was never used as a storehouse, but you get a great view from the top!

Rice growing

Leaving Patna, we travel through a vast rice growing area. Rice was first grown in India around 5,000 years ago. It is still India's most important crop.

India is the world's second-biggest producer of rice, after China. It produces about a fifth of the world's rice. Much of India's rice is consumed at home, but one variety, basmati rice, is an important **export**. India exports about 650,000 tonnes of basmati rice a year.

▼ **Rice is still harvested by hand in many villages along the Ganges.**

River dolphins

As we drift downstream we look out for the Ganges river dolphin. This mammal grows to 2.5 metres long and has a grey-brown skin. It feeds on fish and shellfish, which it snaps up in its long snout.

This dolphin is almost blind. It tracks its prey in the murky water using sound: a system called echolocation. It makes clicking sounds which spread through the water, and bounce back off its prey.

Ganges dolphins are in danger of dying out. Fishing, pollution, boat traffic and irrigation schemes have all reduced their numbers. Only a few thousand are left in the wild.

Silk City

About 200 kilometres downstream from Patna we reach Bhagalpur. This city is so famous for silk production that it is called 'Silk City'. Silk fibre comes from silk moth caterpillars which spin the silk for their **cocoons**. They live on mulberry bushes.

In Bhagalpur, silk is still produced using traditional methods. Workers collect the silk moth cocoons from wild mulberry bushes and dry them in the sun. The cocoons are plunged into boiling water to soften the gum that binds the fibres. Then a skilled worker, called a reeler, unwinds the fibres from several cocoons and joins them to make a long strand

▲ **A worker spins silk on a hand loom.**

◀ **A reeler unwinds silk from moth cocoons. You can see the cocoons in a bag.**

▶ **Washed and dyed silk is hung up to dry in the sun.**

of silk. The thread can now be woven into silk fabric. In Bhagalpur, silk is mainly woven using hand looms. There are only a few power looms in the city. The fabric is then washed, dyed and sold.

Silk production in India has grown quickly in recent years. India now produces more silk than any other country except China. Most of the silk comes from silk farms, where the moths are reared. Only in a few places, such as Bhagalpur, are cocoons still collected from the wild.

The East India Company

Silk was one of the products that attracted British traders to India in the 1600s. The British government formed a trading company called the East India Company to control British interests in eastern Asia.

The company became rich and powerful. It took over other trading companies and gradually controlled most of India. It even had its own army! But in 1784, the British government decided to take control of Indian affairs. The company became less powerful and was closed down in the 1850s.

Kolkata

Kolkata used to be spelled Calcutta. It lies near the coast on the Hooghly River, which is part of the enormous Ganges delta. We leave the main river to visit this huge city.

Lying between the Indian Ocean and the Ganges, Kolkata has an ideal position for a port. In 1690, the East India Company realised this and decided to develop it. Eighty years later it had become the capital of British-controlled India. Trade is still vital to the city's economy, and it is still one of India's biggest ports.

▼ **This modern bridge over the Hooghly River was built in the 1990s.**

Independence and Partition

By 1900 many Indians wanted independence from Britain. But the independence movement was complicated by differences between Hindu and Muslim leaders. In 1947, India gained independence. But it was split into modern India, a Hindu-dominated state, and Pakistan, a Muslim-dominated state. This division is called Partition. Pakistan itself was later divided when East Pakistan broke away to become Bangladesh in 1971.

Partition caused great upheaval and hardship. Many thousands of Muslims moved from India to West and East Pakistan, and as many Hindus moved to India. The Hindus who left East Pakistan settled in Kolkata, just over the border. Kolkata became very densely populated.

Poverty and slums

Under the British, Kolkata was one of India's richest cities. Now it is one of the poorest. About 15 million people live in the city and its suburbs. Services are limited. A great many people live in slums, with no running water, sewerage or electricity. About a quarter of a million people are homeless and live on the streets.

In the 1940s, a Catholic nun named Mother Teresa began working with the poor of Kolkata. She tried to persuade the Indian government to help them. In 1979, she won the Nobel Peace Prize for her work in Kolkata.

▼ **Kolkata's poorest people live in makeshift shelters on the streets.**

The Farakka Barrage

We make our way back to the Ganges. But our route downstream to Bangladesh is blocked by the Farakka Barrage MAP REF 1. The Indian government built this dam in the 1970s to improve navigation around Kolkata. It is the longest barrage in the world.

The barrage diverted water from the Ganges into the Hooghly River. The increased flow flushed away silt that had built up in the Hooghly River around Kolkata. This allowed bigger ships to call at Kolkata, which helped the Indian economy.

Arguments over water

The Farakka Barrage opened in 1976. But it immediately became the subject of a serious argument between India and Bangladesh. The Bangladeshi government feared that the dam would take vital water from Bangladesh.

▶ **The border crossing between India and Bangladesh. Women wait to meet their friends and family.**

Water shortages along the Ganges would be a disaster for its economy. Experts guessed it would cost Bangladesh up to 500 million US dollars a year. Farming, fishing, industry and navigation would all be badly hit.

Some experts also believed that if India opened the barrage when the water level was high, it would cause terrible flooding in Bangladesh. Since 1977, the two countries have signed several agreements over India's use of the Farakka Barrage. The first agreements did not last long, but in 1996 the two finally signed a lasting agreement.

▼ **The Farakka Barrage has a road on top for traffic to use.**

Working together

India and Bangladesh now cooperate to share and manage the Ganges and other rivers in the region. This partnership is vital to the region's future, as the population rises and the need for water increases.

◀ **Trucks wait to cross the border between India and Pakistan.**

We arrange a ride on a fishing boat and head for Bangladesh, on the last stage of our journey.

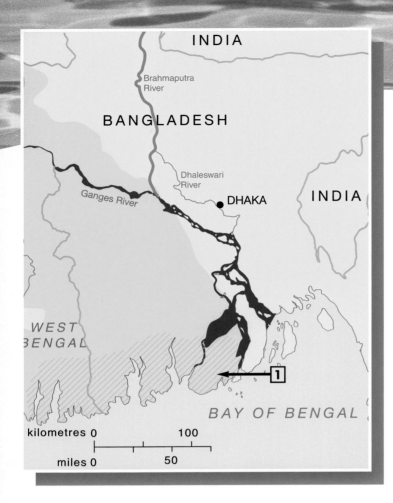

5. The Ganges delta

We leave India and enter Bangladesh. The people of Bangladesh rely on the Ganges to water their crops. However, flooding along the river can bring great danger. We reach the place where another great river, the Brahmaputra, joins the Ganges. The two form the world's biggest delta. Finally we watch as the Ganges flows into the ocean.

▼ **A Bangladeshi farmer harvests jute, an important local crop.**

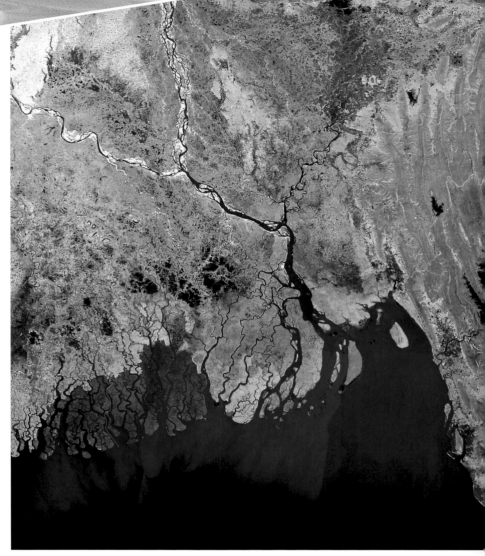

▶ **This satellite image shows the Ganges and its many channels flowing through the delta to the Bay of Bengal.**

A giant delta

About 200 kilometres downstream from Farakka, the Brahmaputra River meets the Ganges. Like the Ganges, this river began high in the Himalayas, tumbling down steep slopes. However, both rivers are now flowing slowly. Because the **current** is slow they begin to drop the massive load of silt collected on their journeys.

Silt blocks the river's path. It splits into many smaller channels as it makes its way to the ocean. These channels are called **distributaries**. The Ganges has eight main distributaries and hundreds of smaller ones. This vast swampy area covers about 75,000 square kilometres. It is the world's largest delta.

Fertile plains

The Ganges delta is very densely populated. Two-thirds of Bangladesh's population work as farmers, raising crops on these flat, fertile lands. Jute is the main crop grown for export. It is used to make twine and sacking. Rice, tea, wheat, sugar cane and fruit are also grown to provide local food and also sell abroad.

Farmers rely on the annual floods to spread fertile silt over their fields. But severe floods can be very dangerous, sweeping away crops, animals, and even homes. People build their homes on stilts or raised banks to guard against flooding.

Monsoon floods

Living in the path of the Ganges is a risky business. An extra long or heavy monsoon can bring disaster, no matter how carefully people prepare. Sometimes the Ganges floods so badly it covers two-thirds of Bangladesh. It causes billions of dollars of damage, and hundreds of people die.

The worst flood in recent history struck in 1998. Around 1,000 people died, and 30 million homes were destroyed.

▼ **Pedal-powered rickshaws struggle through a flood in Bangladesh.**

The floods lasted over two months. The whole rice crop was ruined. The Bangladeshi government had to ask for 900 million US dollars in aid to help feed and shelter its people.

Dhaka and the poor

Dhaka is the capital of Bangladesh. Over eight million people live here. Many are very poor. An organisation called the Grameen Bank, based in Dhaka, helps poor people. The Grameen Bank was founded in 1976 to help poor villagers borrow money and start up businesses.

▲ **The Grameen Bank has now loaned more than I billion US dollars to its members, who are mainly women.**

The Grameen Bank

Since the 1970s, the Grameen Bank has helped about 2.4 million people. Over 90 per cent of its members are women. Ordinary banks refused to lend them money because they were poor. The Grameen Bank has now expanded its role to help the poor. It supports village industries such as weaving and fishing. It also provides services such as a telephone system and the Internet. It is so successful that it has now been copied in over 40 other countries, including India.

Rich in gas

Bangladesh's natural resources include large stocks of natural gas. The gas lies underground in the delta, and also offshore in the Bay of Bengal. Natural gas was discovered here in the 1990s. Several major oil companies were involved in drilling for gas.

The most important gas field, the Sangu, lies offshore. It began production in 1998. The gas produces electricity for light, cooking and industry. It is also used to fuel vehicles and produce fertiliser. Experts believe that huge reserves of natural gas still lie underground in this region.

▲ **A village on the edge of the Sundarbans.**

◀ **The Bengal tiger is the world's most powerful cat.**

wildlife, including some very rare creatures. The estuarine crocodile, Indian python and Bengal tiger live here.

Tourists come to the Sundarbans to catch a glimpse of the Bengal tiger. You have to be very lucky to see one, but they can probably see us. Local people say, 'Here the tiger is always watching you!'

Hurricanes and high seas

Very powerful tropical storms called **cyclones** commonly strike here during the monsoon. These giant spinning storms are also called hurricanes. They blow in from the ocean, bringing howling winds and very heavy rain. The spinning

The Sundarbans

We take a small boat to explore the Sundarbans MAP REF 1 . This vast area of forest and swamp covers 54 islands in the Ganges delta, by the coast. Very few people live here. The area is left to winds suck up seawater. This produces a mound of water called a storm surge. When the storm surge hits land, it acts like a very high tide, causing coastal flooding.

The Sundarbans helps to protect the rest of Bangladesh from cyclones. This vast marshy area absorbs storm waters like a sponge. However, very severe storms break through the natural barrier to cause terrible flooding.

In 1970, an incredibly powerful cyclone hit Bangladesh and half a million people died. In 1991, another terrible cyclone killed 139,000 people and destroyed millions of homes. A storm surge up to six metres high swept inland for 14 kilometres.

After 1991, the Bangladeshi government built concrete storm shelters to protect people from floods. The shelters have been built on stilts safe from the flood water.It also built an early warning system. The new system seems to work. In 1997, another severe storm hit Bangladesh, but killed less than 50 people.

◄ **After 1991, cyclone shelters were built in areas at risk of flooding.**

▼ **A cyclone destroyed these homes on the delta.**

Shrimp and salmon

We leave the marshy Sundarbans and continue our journey by fishing boat. Fishing has been an important industry here for centuries. We head out to where the salt waters of the Indian Ocean mingle with the freshwater of the Ganges. The semi-salty water here is ideal for fish farming. Shrimp and fish such as salmon are reared in cages hanging in the open water.

▶ **Fish drying by the ocean. Drying is a cheap way of preserving fish.**

Rising waters

The greatest threat Bangladesh faces in future is probably **global warming**. This gradual warming of the Earth's surface is happening because of increased amounts of carbon dioxide and certain other gases in the atmosphere. Ice in the polar regions has started to melt because of global warming. If this continues, melting ice would swell the water in the oceans, which would make sea levels rise. Experts guess that sea levels could rise by 0.5 metres by 2100. That may not sound much, but if it happens, much of low-lying Bangladesh could end up underwater.

▼ **A fisherman casts his net into the delta. However fish farming is replacing traditional methods of fishing.**

Journey's End

We have reached the end of our journey along the sacred River Ganges. We have experienced the variety of peoples and places along the river. Now you know all about the Ganges, you can follow the river's fortunes in future.

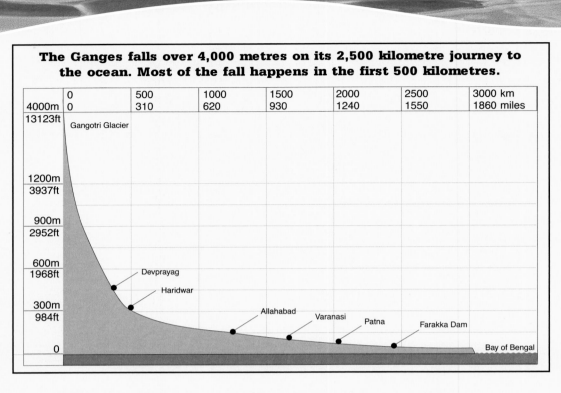

The Ganges falls over 4,000 metres on its 2,500 kilometre journey to the ocean. Most of the fall happens in the first 500 kilometres.

4000m	0	500	1000	1500	2000	2500	3000 km
13123ft	0	310	620	930	1240	1550	1860 miles

Gangotri Glacier

1200m
3937ft

900m
2952ft

600m
1968ft — Devprayag

Haridwar

300m
984ft — Allahabad Varanasi Patna Farakka Dam

0 — Bay of Bengal

Further information

Useful websites

http://templenet.com/Ganga/ganga.html

A website that gives information about the myths, legends and interesting places along the Ganges River.

http://library.thinkquest.org/22659/page2.htm

This website takes you on a virtual tour along the Ganges River, and provides information about places of interest and people living along the river banks.

http://virtualbangladesh.com/bd_tour.html

A website with facts and figures about Bangladesh, which takes on your an online tour of the country.
Learn all about Bangladesh, its people and their way of life.

Books

Celebrate: India by Robyn Hardyman (Watts, 2009)

Countries in the News: India by Anita Ganeri (Watts, 2009)

Fact at your Fingertips: Asia by Derek Hall (Wayland, 2008)

Geography Detective: Rivers by Jen Green (Wayland, 2006)

Geography Now: Rivers around the World by Jen Green (Wayland, 2008)

World in Focus: India by A Brownlie Bojang and N Barber (Wayland 2006)

Glossary

aqueduct a bridge used to carry water.

barrage a dam across a river that holds or diverts water.

canal an artificial waterway.

caste one of the social groups into which Hindu society is traditionally divided.

cholera a disease of the gut.

climate the long-term weather pattern in a region.

cocoon the silken case woven by a caterpillar before it turns into a moth or butterfly.

confluence a place where rivers meet.

current a regular flow of water in a certain direction.

cyclone another name for a hurricane – a huge spinning tropical storm.

dam a barrier that diverts or holds back water.

deforestation loss of forests.

delta a flat, swampy area of land that forms as a river drops silt at its mouth.

distributary one of many channels into which some rivers divide as they approach the sea.

earthquake when rocks shift and crack because of enormous pressure below ground.

echolocation a system used by animals such as bats and dolphins to locate their prey using sound.

ecotourism a type of tourism that aims to protect the environment.

environment the surroundings in which plants, animals and people live.

erosion when rocks and soil are worn away by rain, wind, frost or ice.

export to sell a product abroad, or a product that is sold abroad.

fold mountain a mountain that formed by a collision between two of the huge plates that form Earth's surface.

ghat a stepped stone platform by a river, that people use to reach the water.

global warming warming temperatures worldwide, caused by pollution in the atmosphere.

gorge a deep, narrow valley with sheer sides.

headwaters all the water near the source of a river.

hindi one of the main Indian languages.

hydroelectricity electricity that is made using energy from fast-flowing water.

intercropping when different crops are grown together.

irrigate to water fields with water channelled from a river or stream.

junction a place where roads, rivers or railways join.

landslide when a huge mass of rock and soil slides downhill.

meltwater water produced by melting snow and ice.

monsoon a wind that changes direction through the year, bringing rain at certain times.

navigation the passage of ships and boats.

nirvana the state of bliss that Hindus and Buddhists aim to achieve through meditation.

nomad a person who has no fixed home, but moves from place to place.

nutrients nourishment.

preserve to save.

pulses seed crops such as peas, beans and lentils.

rapids an area of white water where a river crashes over rocks.

reservoir an artificial lake used to store water, made by damming a river or stream.

silt fine sand or mud carried along by a river.

solar energy energy from the sun.

source the place where a river begins.

storm surge a mound of water sucked up by the whirling winds of a hurricane.

tributary a minor river or stream that joins the main river.

turbine a machine powered by steam or water that is used to produce electricity.

typhoid A disease caused by polluted food or water.

Index

Journey Along a River

Contents of titles in the series:

WAYLAND